OUR SOLAR SYSTEM

NEPTUNE

by Alissa Thie

AMICUS

telescope

storm

Look for these words and pictures as you read.

moon

spacecraft

Look at that blue planet.
It is Neptune!

Neptune is cold. It is far away. It is the last planet in our solar system.

Sun

Mercury

Venus

Earth

Mars

Neptune

Uranus

Saturn

Jupiter

telescope

See the telescope?
You need it to see this planet.

See the storm?
It is the dark blue spot.
It is very windy!

storm

moon

See the moons?
Neptune has 14.
The biggest one is Triton.

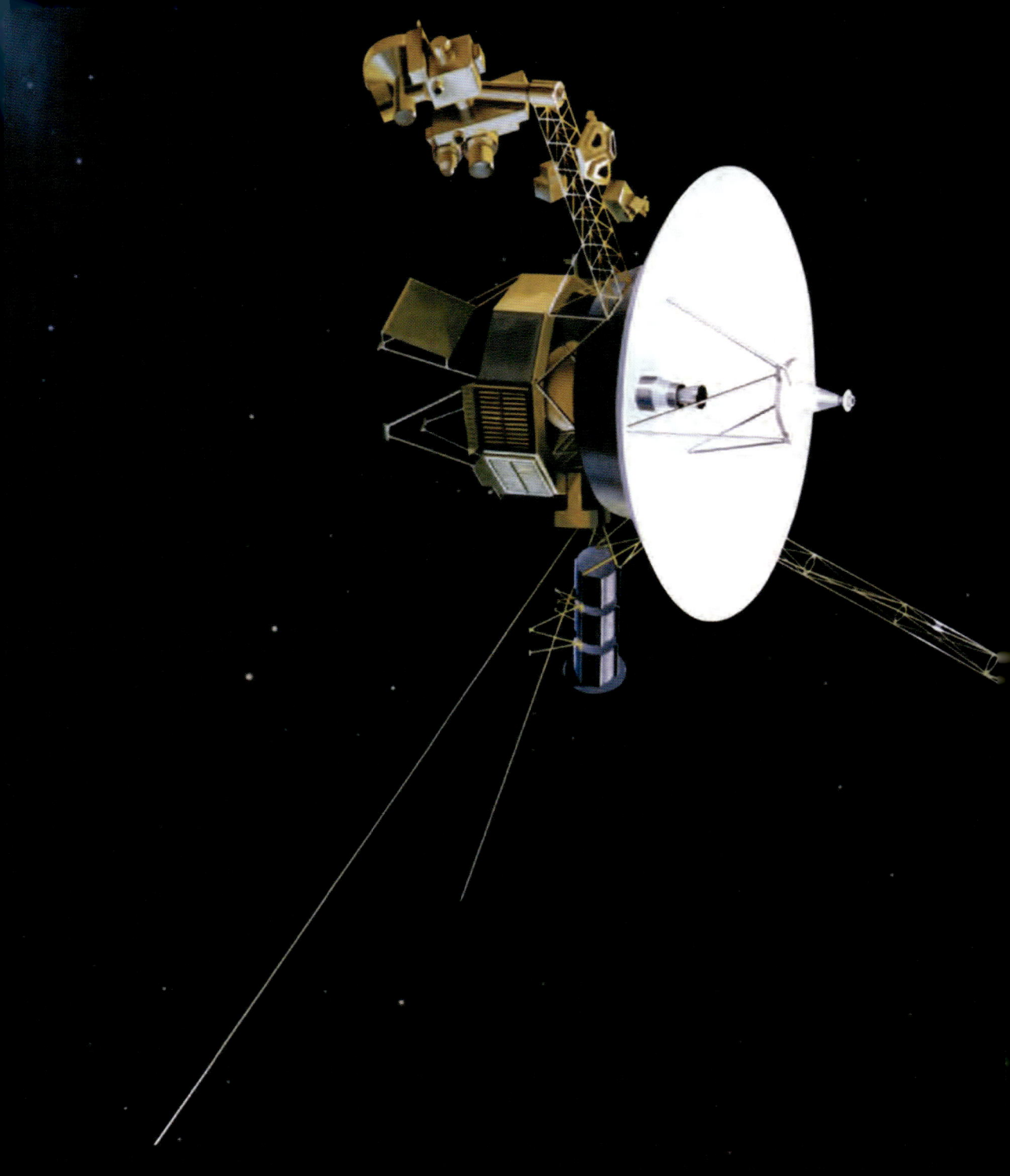

See the spacecraft?
It went to Neptune.
It took pictures.

spacecraft

Are those rings? Yes!
They are thin.

See the telescope?
You need it to see this planet.

telescope

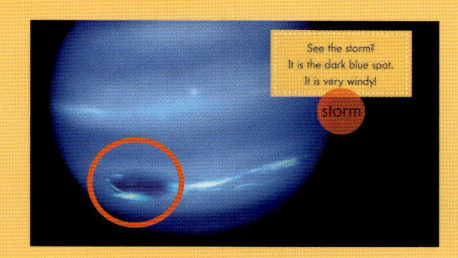

See the storm?
It is the dark blue spot.
It is very windy!

storm

telescope

storm

Did you find?

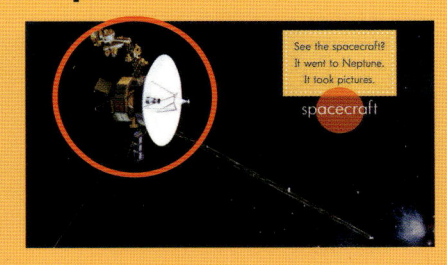

moon

spacecraft

See the moons?
Neptune has 14.
The biggest one is Triton.

moon

See the spacecraft?
It went to Neptune.
It took pictures.

spacecraft

Spot is published by Amicus Learning, an imprint of Amicus
P.O. Box 227, Mankato, MN 56002
www.amicuspublishing.us

Library of Congress Cataloging-in-Publication Data
Names: Thielges, Alissa, 1995– author.
Title: Neptune / by Alissa Thielges.
Other titles: Spot. Our Solar System.
Description: Mankato, MN : Amicus, [2024] | Series: Spot.
    Our Solar System | Audience: Ages 4–7 | Audience:
    Grades K–1 | Summary: "Simple text and a search-and-
    find feature reinforce new science vocabulary about
    Neptune's weather, moons, and thin rings for early
    readers"–Provided by publisher.
Identifiers: LCCN 2022035865 (print) | LCCN 2022035866
    (ebook) | ISBN 9781645492696 (library binding) |
    ISBN 9781681527932 (paperback) |
    ISBN 9781645493570 (ebook)
Subjects: LCSH: Neptune (Planet)—Juvenile literature.
Classification: LCC QB691 .T45 2024 (print) | LCC QB691
    (ebook) | DDC 523.48—dc23/eng20230106
LC record available at https://lccn.loc.gov/2022035865
LC ebook record available at
    https://lccn.loc.gov/2022035866

Printed in China

Rebecca Glaser, editor
Deb Miner, series designer
Lori Bye, book designer
Omay Ayres, photo researcher

Photos by Alamy/dotted zebra 10–11; Getty/
ewg3D 4–5, Science Photo Library—MARK
GARLICK 14, SCIEPRO/SCIENCE PHOTO
LIBRARY cover; iStock/Igor_Filonenko 3;
NASA's Goddard Space Flight Center/JPL/
Mary Pat Hrybyk-Keith 12–13; Shutterstock/
bluecrayola 8–9, Dotted Yeti 1, Pixel-Shot 6–7

NEPTUNE